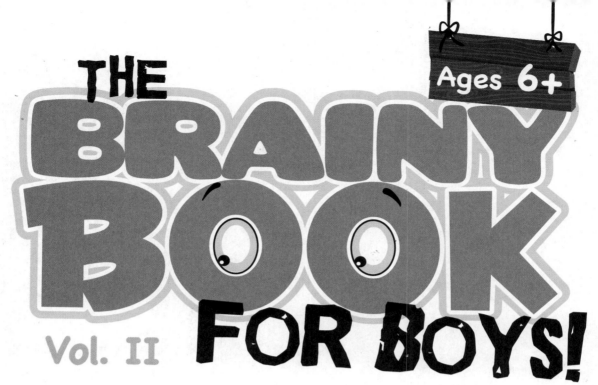

Thinking Kids™
An imprint of Carson-Dellosa Publishing
P.O. Box 35665
Greensboro, NC 27425 USA

Thinking Kids™
An imprint of Carson-Dellosa Publishing LLC
P.O. Box 35665
Greensboro, NC 27425 USA

ISBN 978-1-4838-0701-0

TABLE OF CONTENTS

TABLE OF CONTENTS

Help the dog visit the Seattle Space Needle.

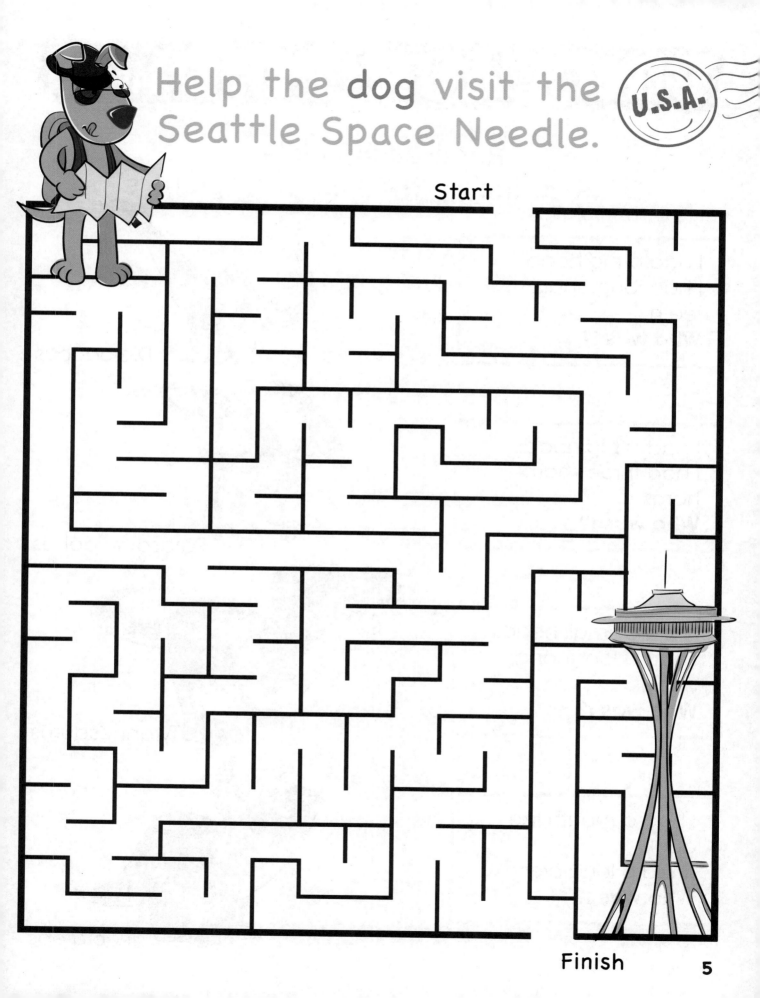

Start

Finish

5

DINOSAUR RIDDLES

Read each riddle.
Draw a line to the matching picture.

I had a big head.
I had long, sharp
teeth.
Who was I?

I had a big head.
I had three sharp
horns.
Who was I?

I had a small head.
I had a long, long
neck.
Who was I?

I had a mouth like a
duck.
I had a long crest.
Who was I?

Diplodocus

Parasaurolophus

Tyrannosaurus

Triceratops

WATCHING WALKERS

What went wandering below?

dRAGON TREASURE HUNT

Find the **23** hidden items in the scene next door.

- Cherry
- Butterfly
- Paperclip
- Golf Club
- Balloon
- Mitten
- Diamond
- Pizza Slice
- Teacup
- Candy Corn
- Heart
- Megaphone
- Glove
- Stamp
- Sock
- Flower Pot
- Umbrella
- Domino
- Leaf
- Flag
- Sailboat
- Banana
- Party Hat

KEYBOARD CRAZY

To find the mystery letter, color the spaces with the following letters green.

N C M E R H F P T B G S A

C	D	L	I	G
T	M	V	Q	H
F	I	P	U	S
A	O	J	B	R
N	V	X	K	E

Circle the mystery letter.   B   K   N

WHAT'S THE DIFF?

One of these things is not like the others.
Can you find the imposter?

CAREER TIME

Use the pictures and words in the word box to help you fill in the puzzle.

1.
2.
3.
4.
5.
6.

doctor
teacher
artist
lawyer
singer
chef

Help the dog visit
the Pyramids of Giza.

Start

Finish

DIFFERENT?

10 differences in these two pictures?

UNSCRAMBLE!

Unscramble each word.
Be sure it goes with the meaning.

One who plays is called a

lapeyr ___ ___ ___ ___ ___ ___ .

A round thing you can kick is a

lalb ___ ___ ___ ___ .

A sweet treat to eat is

danyc ___ ___ ___ ___ ___ .

Something you can win is a

pzire ___ ___ ___ ___ ___ .

A person who wins is the

rnnewi ___ ___ ___ ___ ___ ___ .

One who sails a boat is a

ailsor ___ ___ ___ ___ ___ ___ .

prize
winner
player
ball
sailor
candy

Follow the 🍬's
to get the
kids to the treats!

Start

Finish

TAKE
ONE!

MUNCHY ATTACK!

Read the clues and use the words in the word box to complete the puzzle.

apple	peanut butter	carrots
cherry	cheese	banana

Across
- **3.** It can go in a pie.
- **5.** It is good with jelly.

Down
- **1.** Rabbits like them.
- **2.** It is made from milk.
- **4.** It can be red, yellow, or green.
- **6.** It is yellow and grows in a bunch.

WORD WHEEL

Write the first letter of the words in the puzzle wheel.

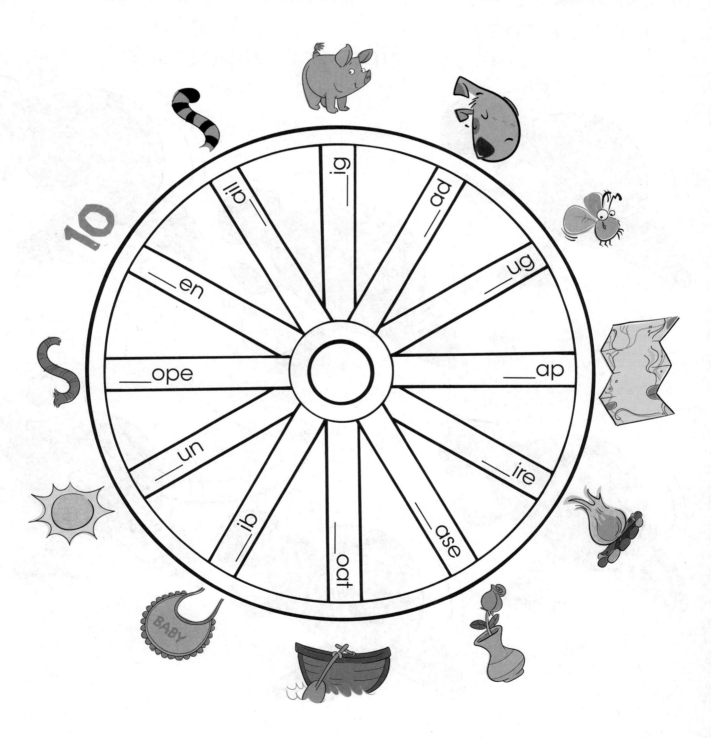

WHAT'S THE DIFF?

One of these things is not like the others.
Can you find the imposter?

BOO!

Find and circle the words in the puzzle.

```
K T A T M A S K I
B G P A R T Y Q M
P A E P X E I N G
I P C F W I A O X
U G J S R O M T E
T C O S T U M E S
R A Y J G G Z L U
Q Z B Q Y Z M E G
```

BAT
COSTUME
MASK
PARTY
TREATS

21

TREE HOUSE TREASURE HUNT

Find the **25** hidden items in the treetop next door.

- ☐ Mitten
- ☐ Leaf
- ☐ Clamshell
- ☐ Ice Cream Cone
- ☐ Envelope
- ☐ Fork
- ☐ Bell
- ☐ Tepee
- ☐ Light Bulb
- ☐ Baseball
- ☐ Fishhook
- ☐ Cup with Straw
- ☐ Mushroom
- ☐ Domino
- ☐ Golf Club
- ☐ Pencil
- ☐ Sock
- ☐ Apple
- ☐ Cherry
- ☐ Top Hat
- ☐ Heart
- ☐ Kite
- ☐ Lollipop
- ☐ Comb
- ☐ Umbrella

MYSTERY PICTURE

Read each sentence and cross out the picture.
What picture is left?

1. It is not a toy.

2. It is not foil.

3. It is not boil.

4. It is not coins.

5. It is not soil.

6. It is not oil.

The mystery picture is a _____ .

ENGLAND

Help the dog visit Big Ben.

Start

Finish

25

COMMUNITY HELPERS

Find and circle the words in the puzzle.

```
w n u r s e p l u m b
d x a z y t e a c h e
o c b c f j a p b l k
c l d a g h u c m d h
t e w u k r q d o e i
o r z v t e s n g f g
r k b u s d r i v e r
```

doctor
nurse
bus driver
clerk
judge
baker

FLY AWAY

Find and circle the words in the puzzle.

```
L P L L V A T J A C
Y J K N T O E W O F
T X L J D G Y C H O
U S I C A A K S W C
G K R G R P J M E E
M E G T I E Y I L V
Z U N T L Q V F G N
L I U S W O L K S F
B L I Y M E V P N W
Z A S T U N A E P C
A D O S O V A C V E
```

AISLE
COCKPIT
LUGGAGE
MOVIE
PEANUTS
SODA

Follow the 's to get the kid to the lunch table!

Finish

28

HOLIDAYS

Write the holidays from the word box in the puzzle.
Then, find the secret word in the purple box.

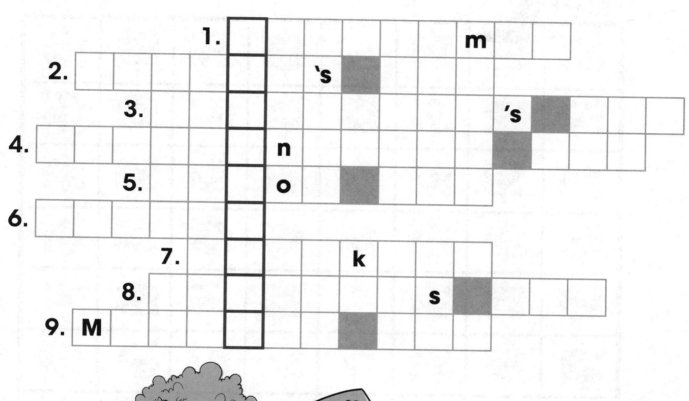

Mother's Day
Father's Day
Veterans Day
Independence Day
Arbor Day
Christmas
Easter
Valentine's Day
Hanukkah

The secret word is _____.

Follow the $'s
to help the
cop catch the robber!

Start

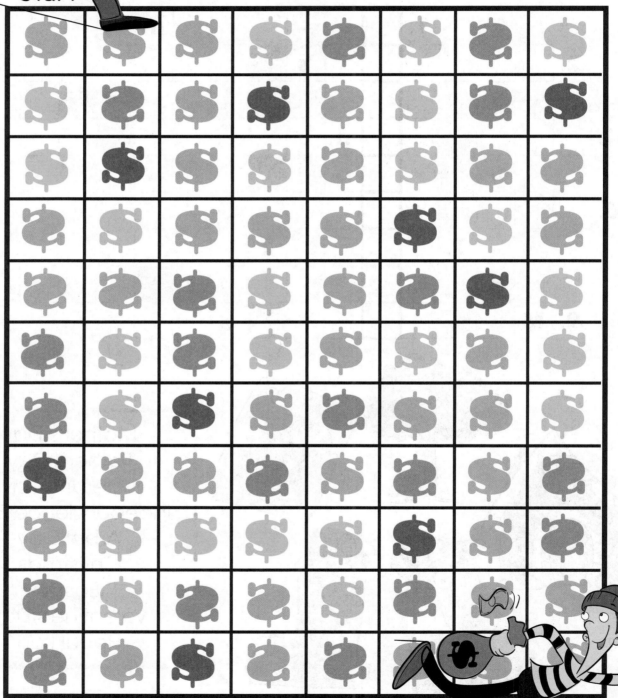

Finish

30

LET'S PLAY

Use the words in the box to help you write the name of each picture.

1. | | | l | |

2. | | i | | |

3. | s | | | | s |

4. | | | g | | |

5. | g | | |

6. | | w | | n | |

7. | | r | | | |

bike

skates

ball

swing

wagon

truck

swim

game

8. | | | | m |

Finish the poster!

AAARRRR!

WANTED

Red Beard the Ragged: Surly Sailor

DRAW 'EM SO'S WE KNOWS HIM

BUILDING HOMES

Find and circle the words in the puzzle.

```
h  i  v  e  s  h  f  c  c  b
o  g  a  n  h  j  t  t  a  r
u  x  r  p  a  l  r  e  z  r
s  k  y  s  c  r  a  p  e  r
e  s  t  b  k  c  i  e  n  e
z  y  c  a  s  t  l  e  u  c
a  p  a  r  t  m  e  n  t  k
u  e  f  t  o  i  r  e  a  s
```

skyscraper
tepee
castle
hive
house
apartment
shack
trailer

ROCK ON!

Design your guitar.

SAIL AWAY

Find and circle the words in the puzzle.

f	a	d	s	t	a	r	b	o
c	n	b	o	o	m	g	z	k
o	c	a	l	w	h	e	e	l
m	h	r	n	t	l	x	m	y
p	o	g	t	g	c	e	a	j
a	r	e	u	n	a	b	s	t
s	h	i	p	p	o	r	t	h
s	p	o	g	k	b	g	l	t

anchor
boom
wheel
compass
ship
barge
port

DIFFERENT?

TRASH OR TREASURE?

What's in the can?

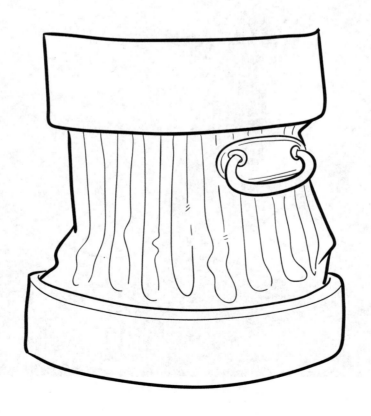

MYSTERY PICTURE

Read each sentence and cross out the picture.
What picture is left?

1. It is not Earth.

2. It is not an astronaut.

3. It is not a rocket ship.

4. It is not a helmet.

5. It is not a alien spaceship.

6. It is not a comet.

7. It is not the moon.

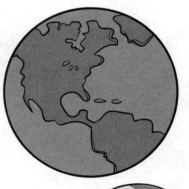

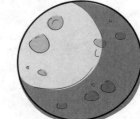

The mystery picture is a _____ .

WHAT'S THE DIFF?

One of these things is not like the others.
Can you find the imposter?

WATER SPORTS

Find and circle the words in the puzzle.

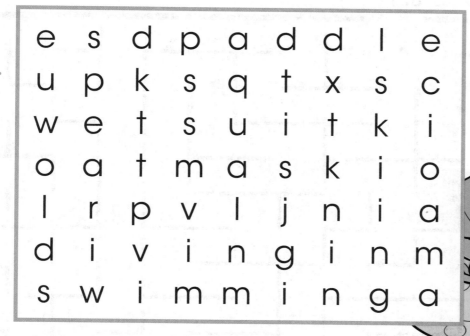

```
e s d p a d d l e
u p k s q t x s c
w e t s u i t k i
o a t m a s k i o
l r p v l j n i a
d i v i n g i n m
s w i m m i n g a
```

skiing	diving
paddle	swimming
mask	wet suit

Draw your favorite water sport!

Help the firetruck get to the kitten stuck in the tree.

Start

Finish

42

GOING PLACES

Read the clues and use the words in the word box to complete the puzzle.

Word Box

airplane
bike
bus
car
truck
boat
balloon

Across
1. It is an automobile.
4. Hot air makes it rise into the sky.
6. This can carry heavy loads on the road.

Down
2. This flies people from city to city.
3. This carries people and big loads on water.
4. It has two wheels and pedals.
5. This takes many people around the city.

MACHINES

Find and circle the words in the puzzle.

```
f d w o u t m t a p j
o m o t o r c y c l e
r e m o v a s l r a t
e s o q w c a r a n p
l a t e e t x r n e u
i w o h i o k j e c e
f f r g d r i l l b c
c o m p u t e r e r h
```

car   saw
plane   tractor
motorcycle   motor
drill   computer
jet

DRAG-GONE

Design the dragon's body.

REPTILES

Find and circle the words in the puzzle.

```
r s n a k e s n a k
c r o c o d i l e z
t o r t o i s e l i
d u w x a k j g i g
e y r v o l n e z u
t s u t p m g c a a
c b r q l f i k r n
s e i n k e h o d a
s i d e w i n d e r
```

turtle
iguana
crocodile
lizard
tortoise
gecko
sidewinder
snake

ANIMAL ANALOGIES

Use the word bank to help complete these analogies. An analogy is the expression of two like comparisons.

| rattlesnake | cow | camel | elephant |

A **hill** is to **land** as a **hump** is to a(n) _____.

A **hand fan** is to a **human** as **ears** are to a(n) _____.

Four quarters are to a **dollar** as **four stomachs** are to a(n) _____.

A **chest beat** is to a **gorilla** as a **shaking rattle** is to a(n)_____.

ALIEN TREASURE HUNT

Find the **29** hidden items in the school bus next door.

- ☐ Slice of Bread
- ☐ Pushpin
- ☐ Shamrock
- ☐ Teacup
- ☐ Seashell
- ☐ Yard Stick
- ☐ Donut
- ☐ Ring
- ☐ Bowl

- ☐ Top Hat
- ☐ Closed Book
- ☐ Magnifying Glass
- ☐ Paperclip
- ☐ Golf Club
- ☐ Pizza Slice
- ☐ Toothbrush
- ☐ Snowman
- ☐ House
- ☐ Envelope

- ☐ Glass
- ☐ Hockey Stick
- ☐ Pencil
- ☐ Flag
- ☐ Smiley Face
- ☐ Basketball
- ☐ Lollipop
- ☐ Banana
- ☐ Mushroom
- ☐ Heart

Finish the front page!

EXTRA!

Dinosaurs in Space!

FISHY CARTOONS

Some fish have names that remind us of other animals. Use the clues to unscramble these fish names. Write each name correctly on the line. Then, use your imagination to draw each fish in a cartoon.

oinlfish
(king of the beasts)

gknifish
(opposite of queen)

rpartofish
(a talking bird)

ogatfish
(a nanny- or a billy-)

Make up your own fish.
Draw it and name it.

Follow the 's to get the RoboChef to the RoboCake!

Start

Finish

WHO OR WHAT?

Read each riddle below. Use the word bank to identify each creative person or product. Write the answer on the line.

I see the world
Containing colors so vast.
With a stroke I preserve
The future, present, and past.

I am a(n) _____ .

My words have tones
From high to low.
They may be uttered
Fast or slow.

I am a(n) _____ .

painter
musician
song
writer

The words I use
May last a long time.
Depending on my talents
They may be prose or rhyme.

I am a(n) _____ .

I can read,
But I don't see letters.
Because of me
The world sounds better.

I am a(n) _____ .

DOUBLE DUTY

Homographs are words that have the same spellings but have different meanings and often different pronunciations. Use the clues to find the missing homographs.

Watch the clam _____**close**_____ its shell _____**close**_____ to the
(shut)   (near)
clownfish.

The prickly porcupine will _____ the _____
(give)   (gift)
to the patient prairie dog.

I _____ the_____ of the whimpering wolf
(wrapped around)   (cut)
with white gauze.

I will _____ a _____ for providing the polar
(predict)   (plan)
bear with polka-dotted pajamas.

UNDERWHATER?

What do you see under the sea?

CRAZY WEATHER

Find and circle the words in the puzzle.

BLIZZARD
ICY
SLEET
SNOWY
STORMY
WINDY

```
D L I A S L E E T F
S J K C G M T W B T
K N Y W Y D I C Q B
E Y O E L Y L L L X
F T J W A O D I D W
J S C Z Y W Z W M I
B I F D A Z H P N N
M M Y R A O M Z G D
S T O R M Y Z O N Y
F E D E D U F Y B H
```

Draw your favorite thing to do in the winter.

THIS 'N' THAT

An analogy is made of two sets of ideas that are compared in the same way. Think how the first set is compared, and compare the second the same way.

Nest is to **bird** as **hive** is to _____ .

Hot is to **cold** as **enemy** is to _____ .

Day is to **night** as **follow** is to _____ .

Paper is to **pencil** as **chalkboard** is to _____ .

Girl is to **boy** as **early** is to _____ .

Help the friends catch some fireflies.

Start

Finish

SECRET MESSAGE

L + (✈ - j) + 's = _____

S + (🐝 - b) = _____

(🌳 - ree) + (🐔 - n) = _____

(🦄 - 🌽) + t + (🛏 - b) = _____

(📎 - pler) + (⬤ - ir) + s = _____

What is your favorite place in the United States?
Draw a picture of it.

BARNYARD TREASURE HUNT

Find the **28** hidden items in the barn next door.

- ☐ Light Bulb
- ☐ Heart
- ☐ Sock
- ☐ Slice of Bread
- ☐ Spoon
- ☐ Soup Can
- ☐ Umbrella
- ☐ Mushroom
- ☐ Sailboat

- ☐ Snail
- ☐ Flowerpot
- ☐ Pizza Slice
- ☐ Glove
- ☐ Stamp
- ☐ Toothbrush
- ☐ Envelope
- ☐ Fishhook
- ☐ Crescent Moon
- ☐ Bell

- ☐ Eyeglasses
- ☐ Comb
- ☐ Candle
- ☐ Lollipop
- ☐ Ice Cream Cone
- ☐ Glass with Straw
- ☐ Needle
- ☐ Ruler
- ☐ Pencil

GRAND CANYON

Complete each fact about the Grand Canyon by unscrambling the letters at the end of each sentence. Use the word bank if necessary.

Mead	desert	Colorado
Arizona	deep	

The canyon is between 4,000 and 5,000 feet _____ .
(epde)

The Grand Canyon is located in northwestern _____ .
(zanioar)

The canyon was formed by the _____ River. (rodoclao)

The bottom of the Grand Canyon is mostly _____ .
(seetrd)

The lake that forms at the southern end of the Grand Canyon is

called Lake _____ . (deam)

What kind of animals do you think live in the Grand Canyon?
Draw a picture of one.

Follow the 🧦's to get the monster under the bed!

Start

Finish

JUMBLED DANGERS

Each set of jumbled letters below represents two possible dangers to explorers. Use the clue to help you unscramble the letters to name the two dangers. Use all the letters, but use each letter only once.

Clue: Both are cats, but one is "king."
PLEIALRONDO

_____   _____

Clue: Both are man-eating and live in or near water.
PIROOEIACCRNDALH

_____   _____

Clue: Both can make you "shake, rattle, and roll."
OEVLCTAUAHEORANQK

_____   _____

Clue: Both like to "monkey around."
BLOBAOIOGRLAN

_____   _____

What is a place you would like to explore?
Draw a picture of this place.

WHAT'S THE DIFF?

One of these things is not like the others.
Can you find the imposter?

SPACE LINGO

Carefully follow each direction on this and the next page to form words that are important for successful space travel.

Write a 3-letter word that means "a rule we must obey." __ __ __

Add the name of the meal you eat at noon. __ __ __ __ __

Remove two letters to form a word that marks the beginning of a space trip. __ __ __ __ __ __

Write a 4-letter word that refers to a bottle stopper. __ __ __ __

Jumble those letters to form a word that means "a stone." __ __ __ __

Add "et" for the power source for a spaceship. __ __ __ __ __ __

Write a 5-letter verb that shows how you might cook turkey or chicken.

__ __ __ __ __

Add a fish often used in sandwiches. __ __ __ __

Jumble the letters and you will have the name of a space crew member.

__ __ __ __ __ __ __ __ __

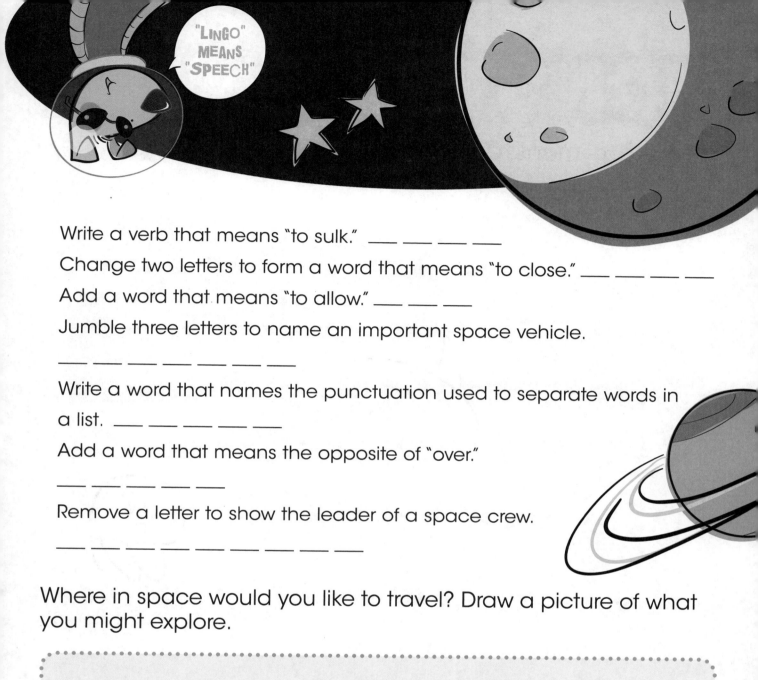

"LINGO" MEANS "SPEECH"

Write a verb that means "to sulk." __ __ __ __

Change two letters to form a word that means "to close." __ __ __ __

Add a word that means "to allow." __ __ __

Jumble three letters to name an important space vehicle.

__ __ __ __ __ __ __

Write a word that names the punctuation used to separate words in a list. __ __ __ __ __

Add a word that means the opposite of "over."

__ __ __ __ __

Remove a letter to show the leader of a space crew.

__ __ __ __ __ __ __ __ __

Where in space would you like to travel? Draw a picture of what you might explore.

MONSTER  MASH

Make a monster out of  these parts.

SURPRISE!

Use the key to figure out the code and unscramble the answer to the question.

What has two heads, twenty-four legs and sharp, pointy teeth?

KEY	
A	1
B	2
D	3
G	4
H	5
I	6
K	7
N	8
O	9
R	10
S	11
T	12
U	13
W	14
Y	15

6

	9	12	3	8

	8	7	9	14

| | | |
| 13 | 12 | 2 |

| | |
| 12 | 6 |

| | |
| 11 | 6 |

	1	6	12	8	4	8	11	3

| | |
| 8 | 6 |

| | | |
| 13 | 15 | 10 | 9 |

| | | |
| 6 | 5 | 1 | 10 |

QUICK AND EZ

I was so tired last night I took some shortcuts with my homework. Today, I have to do it all over again the right way. Can you help me rewrite each sentence as it should be?

4T pounds of honE had the B's in XTC.

_____

Y do U NV the NRG of an electric EL?

_____

The AV8R flew the jet in XS of 4T5 hundred mph.

_____

I threw salt on the IC sidewalk.

_____

Draw a picture to show one of the sentences.

Help the player take his shot.

Start

Finish

SPOOKY

Find and circle the words in the puzzle.

```
B  P  M  Y  X  N  H  U  T  B  F
O  J  J  W  I  T  C  H  R  F  U
O  S  T  F  L  X  R  E  Y  F  L
C  T  B  L  A  C  K  C  A  T  L
N  C  A  N  D  Y  M  Y  E  N  M
A  D  K  T  U  B  R  R  I  E  O
S  K  E  L  E  T  O  N  A  K  O
E  Z  H  X  N  A  H  L  C  C  N
```

SKELETON   FULL MOON
BOO   CANDY
WITCH   BLACK CAT

Draw something spooky.

Finish the poster!

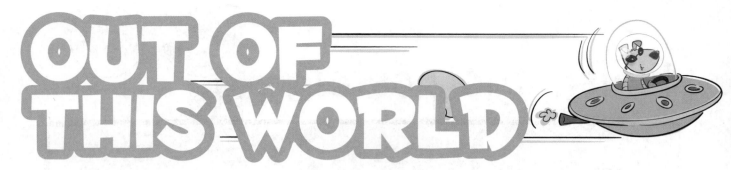

OUT OF THIS WORLD

Design an alien space craft.

Help the matador reach his bull.

Start

Finish

RIDDLE TIME

Use the word box on the next page to answer each clue in the squares on the right. Then, use your answers to fill in the letters of the riddle on the next page.

a. Not old

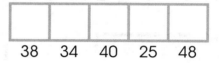

38 34 40 25 48

b.  and thank you

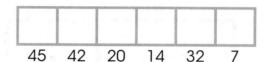

45 42 20 14 32 7

c. Police _____

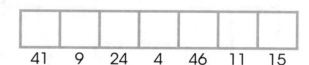

41 9 24 4 46 11 15

d. Tells the time

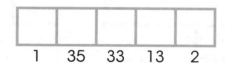

1 35 33 13 2

e. You smell with this

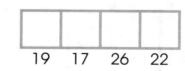

19 17 26 22

f. Long stream of water

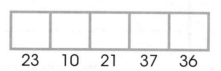

23 10 21 37 36

g. Female nobility

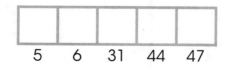

5 6 31 44 47

76

h. What you do with a paddle

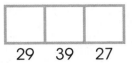

29 39 27

i. Japanese currency

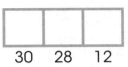

30 28 12

j. You don't _____? (rhymes with "hay")

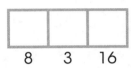

8 3 16

k. Second and last vowels in the
   alphabet, not including "y"

43 18

watch	please
river	EU
yen	nose
young	station
queen	say
row	

‾1‾ ‾2‾ ‾3‾ ‾4‾   ‾5‾ ‾6‾ ‾7‾ ‾8‾ ‾9‾ ‾10‾ ‾11‾ ‾12‾   ‾13‾ ‾14‾ ‾15‾

‾16‾ ‾17‾ ‾18‾   ‾19‾ ‾20‾ ‾21‾ ‾22‾ ‾23‾   ‾24‾ ‾25‾ ‾26‾ ‾27‾ ‾28‾ ‾29‾

"‾30‾ ‾31‾ ‾32‾"   ‾33‾ ‾34‾?

"‾35‾ ‾36‾ ‾37‾   ‾38‾ ‾39‾ ‾40‾   ‾41‾ ‾42‾ ‾43‾ ‾44‾ ‾45‾ ‾46‾ ‾47‾ ‾48‾?"

AHOY!

Find and circle the words in the puzzle.

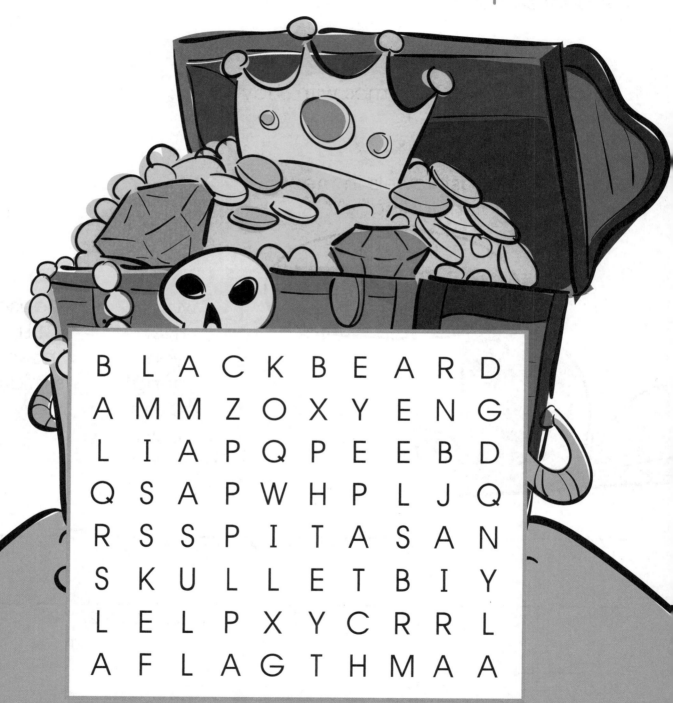

```
B L A C K B E A R D
A M M Z O X Y E N G
L I A P Q P E E B D
Q S A P W H P L J Q
R S S P I T A S A N
S K U L L E T B I Y
L E L P X Y C R R L
A F L A G T H M A A
```

MAP   FLAG
EYEPATCH   SKULL   BLACKBEARD

WILD WEST

Use the word list to fill out the grid below.
Hint: Count the squares in the grid first to
see where the words will fit.

3-Letters	4-Letters	5-Letters	6-Letters	7-Letters
map	pipe	range	cowboy	sheriff
aim	spur	sheep	cactus	rawhide
			cattle	
			saloon	

g h o s t t o w n

p
r
a
i
r
i
e

SURF'S UP TREASURE HUNT

Find the **24** hidden items in the ocean next door.

- ☐ Mushroom
- ☐ Crown
- ☐ Lollipop
- ☐ Crescent Moon
- ☐ Can of Soup
- ☐ Carrot
- ☐ Heart
- ☐ Bowl with Spoon
- ☐ Bendy Straw
- ☐ Sock
- ☐ Spool of Thread
- ☐ Magnifying Glass

- ☐ Leaf
- ☐ Lemon Slice
- ☐ Pencil
- ☐ Smiley Face
- ☐ Rainbow Cloud
- ☐ Banana
- ☐ Popsicle
- ☐ Feather
- ☐ Pear
- ☐ Paintbrush
- ☐ Horseshoe
- ☐ Glove

WHAT'S THE DIFF?

One of these things is not like the others.
Can you find the imposter?

Design your custom bike.

MOTOR MAKER

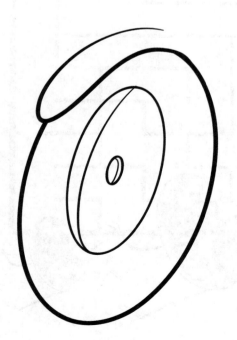

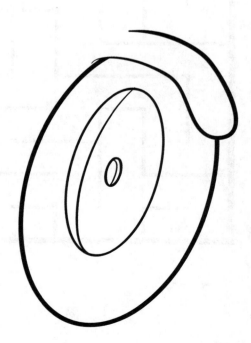

Help the elephant get some peanuts.

Start

Finish

BRRR!

Use the word lists to fill out the grid below.
Hint: Count the squares in the grid first to
see where the words will fit.

3-Letters
ice
ski

4-Letters
cold
melt

5-Letters
sleet
spill
parka

6-Letters
skated

7-Letters
shivers

m i t t e n s

DRAGONS

Find and circle the words in the puzzle.

D J W J D M Y T H T
Y R C S A C K M B O
G O A P O W E R F V
U T G G A A M L L B
V R K E O Q L E A A
M R C T M N G B M R
F I E R C E V L E J
L E R M Y L Y B U S

POWER
DRAGON
FLAME
MYTH
FIERCE

86

WHOSE NOSE?

Do you know who goes with each nose?

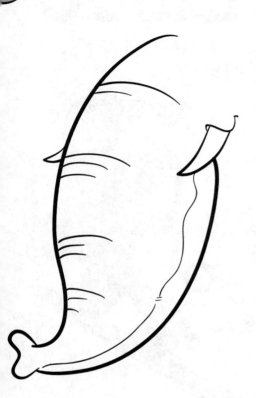

WHAT'S THE DIFF?

One of these things is not like the others.
Can you find the imposter?

THAT'S LOUD!

Find and circle the words in the puzzle.

C O S U D X A W A
R Z Z G A B H K S
A S F D N I O C C
S J I E S A R O N
H T R T L E B X M
F U L K A G R B R
Q E U M R O A R A
X E I M A O T I N

BANG
BOOM
CRASH
ROAR
SCREAM
WHISTLE

Draw something that's loud.

WHAT'S

Can you spot and circle the

DIFFERENT?

10 differences in these two pictures?

Finish the poster!

WANTED

Jesse Longhorn the Big Bad Bull

DRAW 'EM SO'S WE KNOWS HIM

WHAT'S THE DIFF?

One of these things is not like the others.
Can you find the imposter?

Help the **sweaty swimmer** to the kiddie pool.

Start

Finish

94

ALIENS!

Find and circle the words in the puzzle.

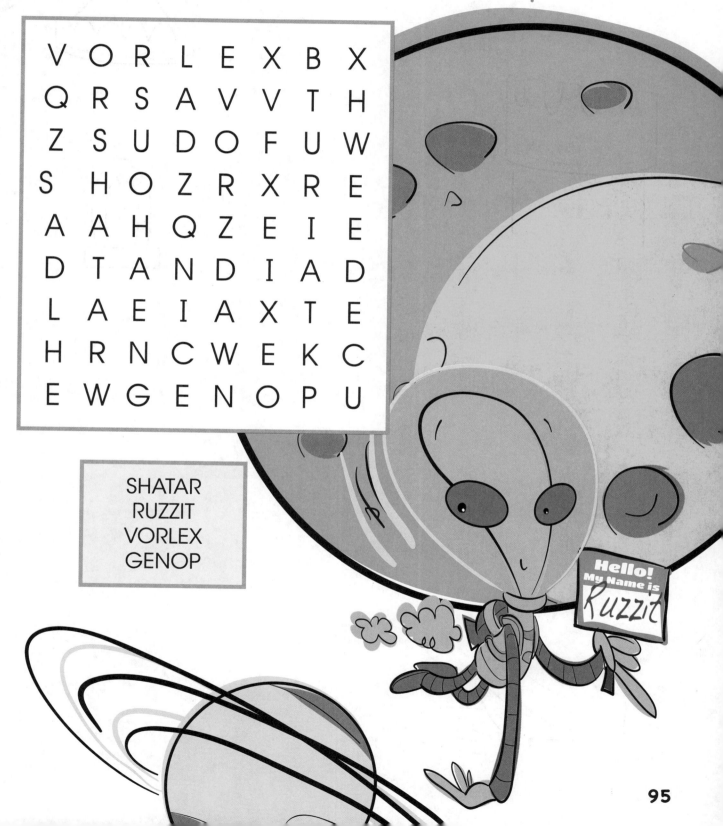

```
V O R L E X B X
Q R S A V V T H
Z S U D O F U W
S H O Z R X R E
A A H Q Z E I E
D T A N D I A D
L A E I A X T E
H R N C W E K C
E W G E N O P U
```

SHATAR
RUZZIT
VORLEX
GENOP

Doodle the rest of the castle.

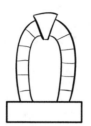

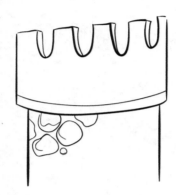

WHAT'S THE DIFF?

One of these things is not like the others.
Can you find the imposter?

OUT IN SPACE

Find and circle the words in the puzzle.

SOLAR
SUN
SYSTEM
URANUS
VENUS

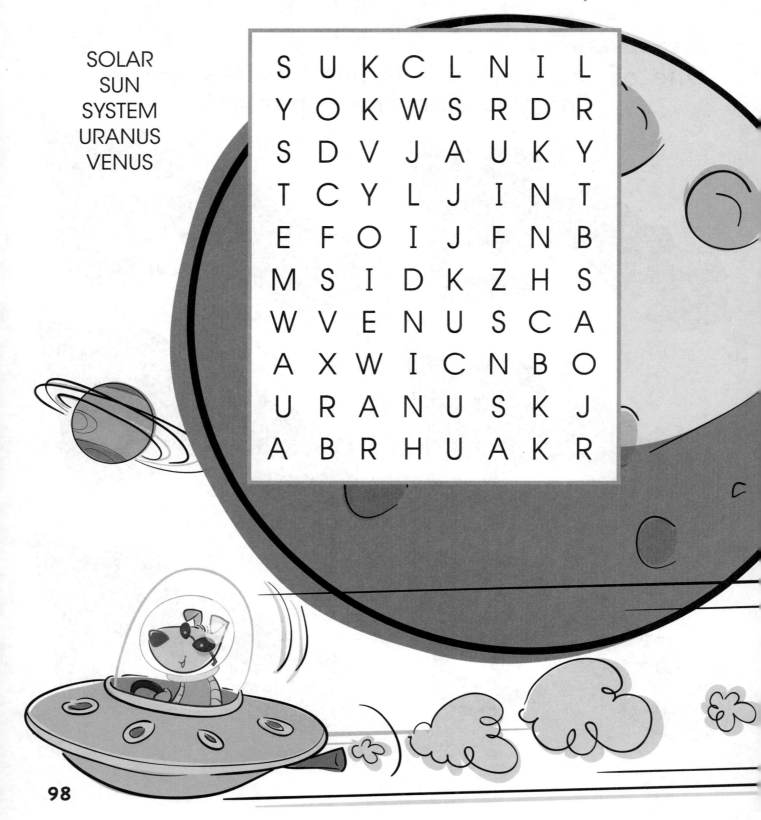

S U K C L N I L
Y O K W S R D R
S D V J A U K Y
T C Y L J I N T
E F O I J F N B
M S I D K Z H S
W V E N U S C A
A X W I C N B O
U R A N U S K J
A B R H U A K R

Finish the poster!

LOST

CITY ZOO

Use the word lists to fill out the grid below.
Hint: Count the squares in the grid first to
see where the words will fit.

3-Letters
cub
pet

4-Letters
cage
deer

5-Letters
tiger
teeth

6-Letters
snakes
safari

7-Letters
habitat
peanuts

8-Letters
elephant

HOT STUFF

Find and circle the words in the puzzle.

V	E	R	U	G	Z	U	M
S	O	F	F	I	R	E	M
T	D	L	A	P	H	I	U
E	O	A	O	K	S	R	S
A	C	V	F	A	P	O	W
M	A	A	U	C	A	N	L
T	A	N	E	V	O	T	S
J	A	V	A	E	P	S	L
V	O	L	C	A	N	O	R

FIRE   STEAM
IRON   VOLCANO
LAVA

Draw something that is hot.

DINO DIG TREASURE HUNT

Find the **25** hidden items in the scene next door.

- ❑ Human Tooth
- ❑ Kite
- ❑ Cane
- ❑ Lemon Slice
- ❑ Piece of Popcorn
- ❑ Smiley Face
- ❑ Key
- ❑ Mushroom
- ❑ Bell
- ❑ Light Bulb
- ❑ Bowl
- ❑ Banana

- ❑ Paintbrush
- ❑ Pear
- ❑ Leaf
- ❑ Tepee
- ❑ Cracked Egg
- ❑ Stocking
- ❑ Button
- ❑ Heart
- ❑ Sailboat
- ❑ Party Hat
- ❑ Soup Can
- ❑ Paperclip
- ❑ Pizza Slice

Help the alien find his ride.

Start

Finish

104

BUSY YEAR

Use the word lists to fill out the grid below.
Hint: Count the squares in the grid first to
see where the words will fit.

4-Letters
year
moon

5-Letters
month
daily
party

7-Letters
holiday

8-Letters
birthday
meetings

OUTER SPACE

Find and circle the words in the puzzle.

J U P I T E R S

N E P T U N E A

S A E P S T W T

Y P R C O P C U

S E E Y A O A R

A P X E T P N N

P L A N E T S O

SPACE
PLANETS
JUPITER

NEPTUNE
SATURN

SURPRISE!

What's inside?

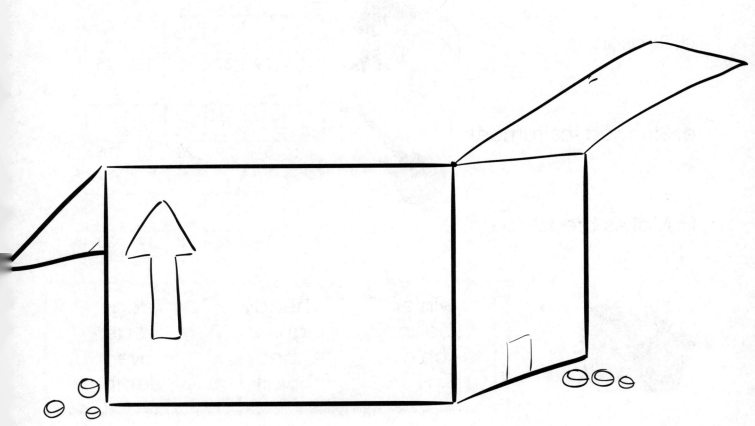

BEAVER CLUES

Use the word box to answer each clue in the squares. Then, use your answers to fill in the letters of the riddle on the next page.

a. Lima _____

11	35	32	43

b. To be patient

45	3	6	8

c. Used to chew food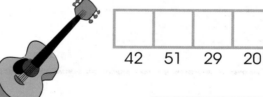

22	41	24	25	2

d. Season

1	39	37	4	12	26

e. Stringed instrument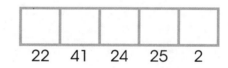

42	51	29	20	13	16

f. Makes bread rise

19	28	18	17	30

winter	heady	dogs
bean	guitar	yeast
chin	bee	oven
H	wait	teeth

108

g. Wanting one's own way

9	15	44	5	49

h. It's below your lips

40	31	46	38

i. Baking appliance

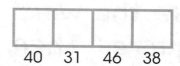

50	14	10	47

j. It's raining cats and ____

7	21	48	33

k. What insect makes honey?

34	27	36

l. Eighth letter of the alphabet

23

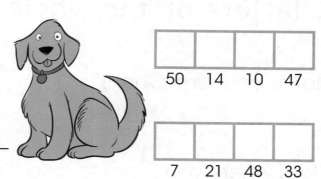

‾1‾ ‾2‾ ‾3‾ ‾4‾   ‾5‾ ‾6‾ ‾7‾   ‾8‾ ‾9‾ ‾10‾   ‾11‾ ‾12‾ ‾13‾ ‾14‾ ‾15‾ ‾16‾

‾17‾ ‾18‾ ‾19‾   ‾20‾ ‾21‾   ‾22‾ ‾23‾ ‾24‾   ‾25‾ ‾26‾ ‾27‾ ‾28‾ ?

‾29‾ ‾30‾   ‾31‾ ‾32‾ ‾33‾   ‾34‾ ‾35‾ ‾36‾ ‾37‾   ‾38‾ ‾39‾ ‾40‾ ‾41‾

‾42‾ ‾43‾ ‾44‾ ‾45‾ ‾46‾ ‾47‾ ‾48‾   ‾49‾ ‾50‾ ‾51‾ !

PIG PEN

Use the word box to answer each clue in the squares. Then, use your answers to fill in the letters of the riddle on the next page.

a. Makes you say, "Ouch!"

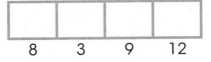
8 3 9 12

b. Class where you learn to add

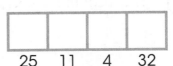
25 11 4 32

c. Where bees live

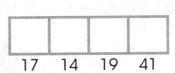
17 14 19 41

d. Hospital room with a TV and magazines

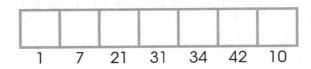
1 7 21 31 34 42 10

e. You bake in it

30 35 20 22

f. Piggy _____

29 18 38 16

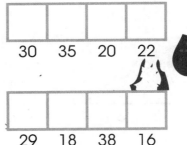

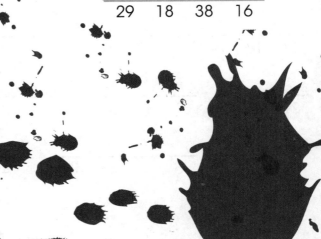

g. Swimming place

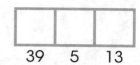
40 24 27 33

h. Opposite of "subtract"

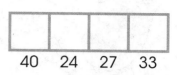
39 5 13

i. It lays eggs

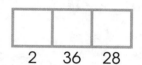
2 36 28

j. A penny is a _____

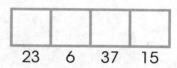
23 6 37 15

k. Thirteenth letter of the alphabet

26

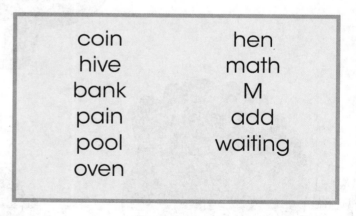

coin   hen
hive   math
bank   M
pain   add
pool   waiting
oven

— — — —   — —   —   — — —   — — —
1 2 3 4   5 6   7   8 9 10   11 12 13

— — —   — — — —   — —   — — — — —   ?
14 15 16   17 18 19 20   21 22   23 24 25 26 27 28

— — — —   — — — —   — —   —   — — —   .
29 30 31 32   33 34 35 36   37 38   39   40 41 42

WHAT'S THE DIFF?

One of these things is not like the others.
Can you find the imposter?

SUMMER FUN

Use the word lists to fill out the grid below.
Hint: Count the squares in the grid first to
see where the words will fit.

3-Letters
hot
tan
run

4-Letters
swim
bike
kite
sail
cone

5-Letters
skate
storm

6-Letters
movies
shorts

icecream

FALL FUN TREASURE HUNT

Find the **23** hidden items in the leaf pile next door.

- ☐ Balloon
- ☐ Teacup
- ☐ Popsicle
- ☐ Pencil
- ☐ Paperclip
- ☐ Mitten
- ☐ Flowerpot
- ☐ Comb
- ☐ Marker
- ☐ Eyeglasses
- ☐ Bowl
- ☐ Heart
- ☐ Worm
- ☐ Bell
- ☐ Mushroom
- ☐ Toothbrush
- ☐ Light bulb
- ☐ Pine Tree
- ☐ Banana
- ☐ Crescent Moon
- ☐ Basketball
- ☐ Carrot
- ☐ Whistle

AAARRGHH!

What scared this kid?

RHYME THIS!

Using the pictures as hints, fill in the missing letters of the rhyming words.

	G	U	M

	S	N	A	K	E

K	I	T	E

WHAT'S THE DIFF?

One of these things is not like the others.
Can you find the imposter?

FOUR SQUARE

Starting with the top word in each square, change one letter at a time until the top word becomes the bottom word.

1.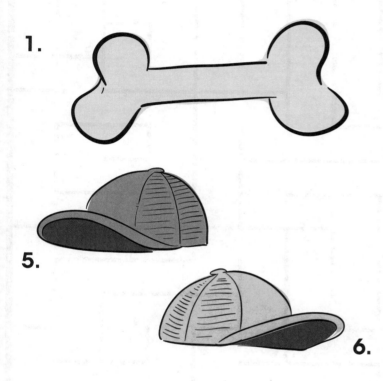

1. B	O	N	E
2.			
3.			
4.			
5. C	A	P	S

5.

6.

6. T	A	L	K
7.			
8.			
9.			
10. D	I	M	E

BLAH, BLAH,!

10.

Race the monster truck to the ramp.

Start

Finish

120

AT THE POOL

Use the word lists to fill out the grid below. Hint: Count the squares in the grid first to see where the words will fit.

3-Letters	**4-Letters**	**5-Letters**	**6-Letters**	**7-Letters**
tan	pool	slide	lotion	whistle
sun	dive	float		
	raft			
	rest			
	laps			

t o w e l

l i f e g u a r d

UP, UP, AND AWAY!

Finish the hero so he can be super!

PIRATES!

Find and circle the words in the puzzle.

```
T Q V I S E S I
C A P T A I N D
F D T P W F C Q
N D B T J J W M
H O O H O O K R
G X O B H O Z H
H D T C O I N S
U I S E L A K E
```

TATTOO
HOOK
CAPTAIN
BOOTS
COINS

Help the Triceratops escape the T-rex.

Start

Finish

LETTER CHANGE

Starting with the top word in each square, change one letter at a time until the top word becomes the bottom word.

1.

5.

1.	R	I	P	E
2.				
3.				
4.				
5.	P	A	L	M

6.

6.	M	I	C	E
7.				
8.				
9.				
10.	L	A	R	K

10.

TECHNO T-REX

Finish up this Robosaurus.

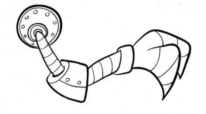

PUZZLE CLUES

Use the pictures as clues to fill in the crossword puzzle.

1 ACROSS

2 ACROSS

1 DOWN

3 DOWN

4 DOWN

5 DOWN

6 ACROSS

7 ACROSS

Help the racer reach the finish line.

Start

Finish

WHAT'S THE DIFF?

One of these things is not like the others.
Can you find the imposter?

FLYIN' HIGH

Design a flag for your own country.

CHANGE A LETTER

Starting with the top word in each square, change one letter at a time until the top word becomes the bottom word.

1.

BREAD
MILK
CHEESE
EGGS

1.	L	I	S	T
2.				
3.				
4.				
5.	M	A	N	E

5.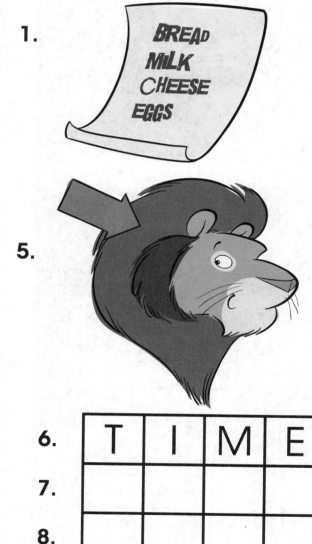

6.

6.	T	I	M	E
7.				
8.				
9.				
10.	F	E	L	L

10.

WHAT'S

Can you spot and circle the

DIFFERENT?

10 differences in these two pictures?

SHARE TWO LETTERS

Each word has two letters in common with the other words. Using the pictures as hints, fill in the rest of the words.

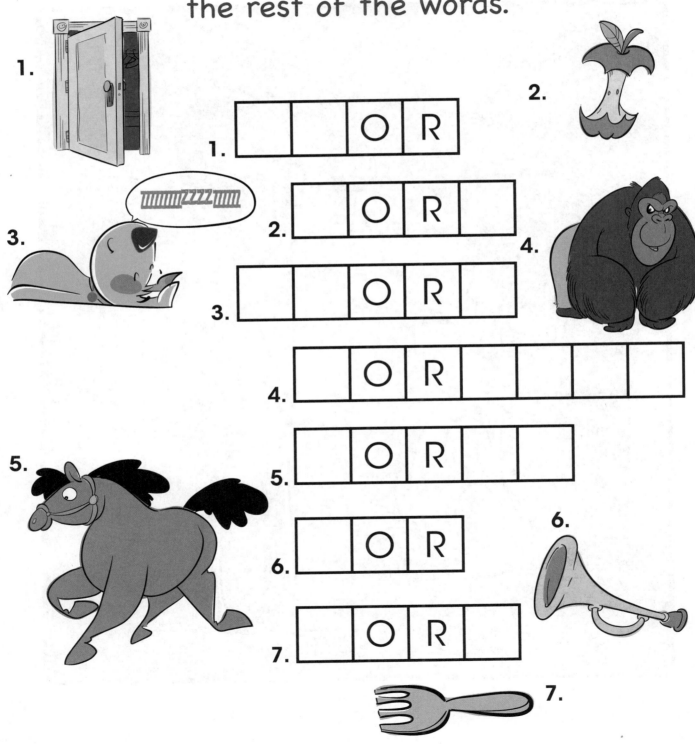

1. [ ] [ ] [O] [R]

2. [ ] [O] [R] [ ]

3. [ ] [ ] [O] [R]

4. [ ] [O] [R] [ ] [ ] [ ]

5. [ ] [O] [R] [ ] [ ]

6. [ ] [O] [R]

7. [ ] [O] [R] [ ]

Get the **pirates** away from the sea monster.

Start

Finish

135

PICTURE CLUES

Use the pictures as clues to fill in the crossword puzzle.

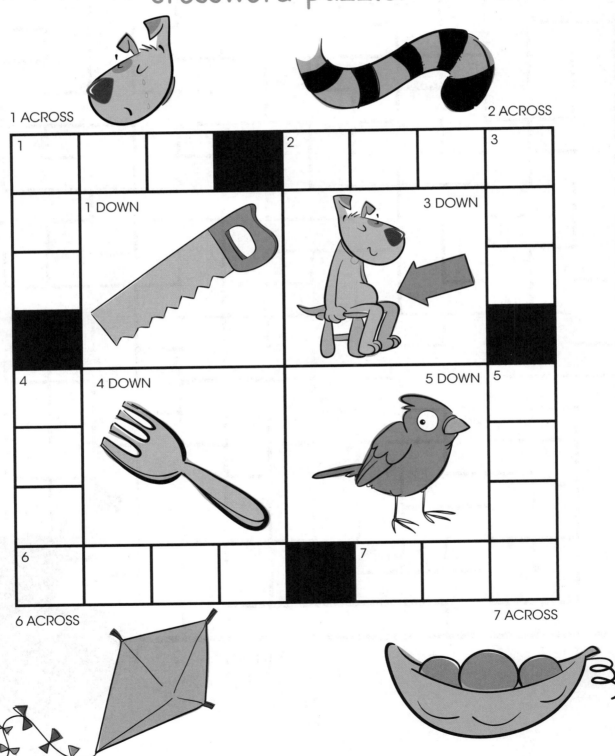

1 ACROSS

2 ACROSS

1 DOWN

3 DOWN

4 DOWN

5 DOWN

6 ACROSS

7 ACROSS

DRAGON NAMES

Find and circle the words in the puzzle.

```
K Q S N R W I S O
T A C M U W C A R
C Q T C A K T P G
Y I G L F U C H W
I Y P Y A Y G I U
M O O N C C F R U
W F G L F I A A S
R G E R R O L R O
```

ERROL
KATLA
MOON
SMAUG
SAPHIRA

GOALIE TREASURE HUNT

Find the **21** hidden items at the soccer field next door.

- [ ] Open Book
- [ ] House
- [ ] Baseball Cap
- [ ] Crayon
- [ ] Flowerpot
- [ ] Flag
- [ ] Ice Cream Cone
- [ ] Arrow
- [ ] Cotton Candy
- [ ] Bendy Straw
- [ ] Heart
- [ ] Comb
- [ ] Fishhook
- [ ] Cherry
- [ ] Paperclip
- [ ] Suspension Bridge
- [ ] Whistle
- [ ] Hockey Stick
- [ ] Domino
- [ ] Pencil
- [ ] Sailboat

SHARE TWO LETTERS

Each word has two letters in common with the other words. Using the pictures as hints, fill in the rest of the words.

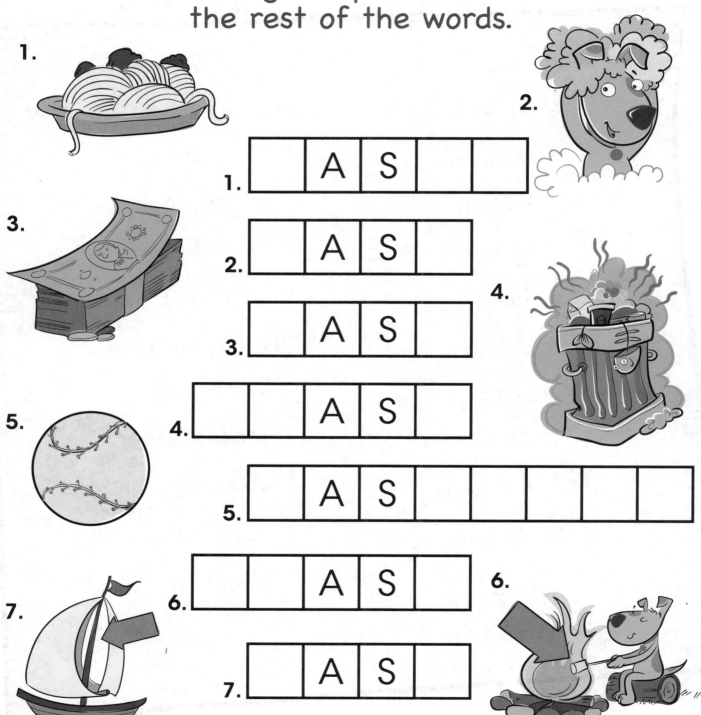

1.

2.

3.

5.

7.

4.

6.

1. [ ] A S [ ] [ ]

2. [ ] A S [ ]

3. [ ] A S [ ]

4. [ ] [ ] A S [ ]

5. A S [ ] [ ] [ ] [ ] [ ]

6. [ ] [ ] A S [ ]

7. [ ] A S [ ]

 ZOMEBODY

...needs a head.
Doodle up this
zombie noggin.

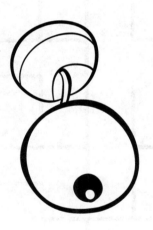

Help the boy escape from the zombies.

Start

Finish

LETTER CHANGE

Starting with the top word in each square, change one letter at a time until the top word becomes the bottom word.

1.

1.	T	O	W	N
2.				
3.				
4.				
5.	D	A	R	T

5.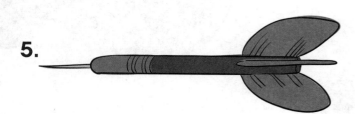

6.

6.	F	A	R	M
7.				
8.				
9.				
10.	T	I	M	E

10.

WHAT'S THE DIFF?

One of these things is not like the others.
Can you find the imposter?

BALLGAME!

Find and circle the words in the puzzle.

```
F  J  M  A  E  T  Z  Z  I  W
P  I  T  C  H  E  R  F  D  G
F  S  H  F  S  W  T  W  P  S
F  T  V  A  U  H  C  G  T  X
U  A  E  D  I  C  C  R  F  Z
O  D  J  R  W  U  I  R  S  C
G  I  D  R  T  K  C  C  T  B
I  U  O  E  E  A  W  A  E  S
C  M  C  A  T  C  H  E  R  O
```

CATCHER	STRIKE
PITCHER	TEAM
STADIUM	THIRD

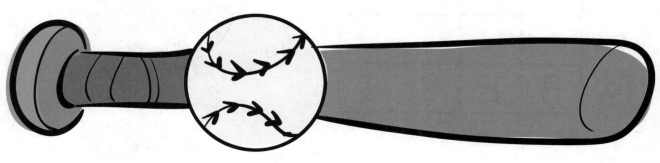

NEW WORDS

Starting with the top word in each square, change one letter at a time until the top word becomes the bottom word.

1.

5.

1.	C	A	P	E
2.				
3.				
4.				
5.	F	I	N	S

6.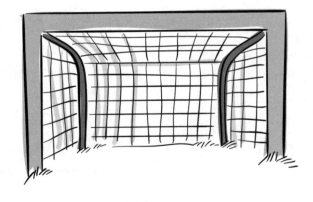

6.	G	O	A	L
7.				
8.				
9.				
10.	B	E	S	T

10.

RHYME THIS!

Using the pictures as hints, fill in the missing letters of the rhyming words.

F	I	S	H

K	N	E	E

R	O	A	C	H

DIFFERENT?

10 differences in these two pictures?

SPACE!

Use the word lists to fill out the grid below.
Hint: Count the squares in the grid first to
see where the words will fit.

4-Letters
Mars
star

5-Letters
Venus
Pluto
Titan
comet

6-Letters
Uranus

7-Letters
Jupiter
Neptune

8-Letters
Milky Way

A S T E R O I D

WHOSE NOSE?

Do you know who goes with each nose?

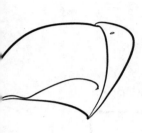

PICTURE CLUES

Use the pictures as clues to fill in the crossword puzzle.

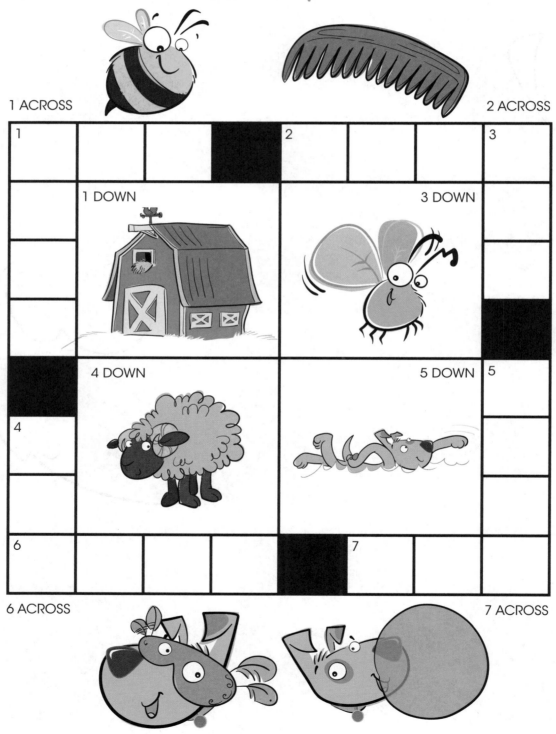

1 ACROSS

2 ACROSS

1 DOWN

3 DOWN

4 DOWN

5 DOWN

6 ACROSS

7 ACROSS

152

REALLY BIG

Find and circle the words in the puzzle.

```
I  M  Q  E  O  W  C  P  M  F  V  I
M  K  A  F  Z  Y  G  O  H  Z  Z  Q
M  K  L  S  L  B  N  Y  S  Y  H  Z
E  L  V  L  S  T  G  Y  T  Y  H
N  W  A  M  T  I  Q  Q  K  H  K  U
S  R  V  R  B  J  V  X  L  G  E  G
E  T  O  B  H  B  P  E  S  I  S  E
B  U  L  E  R  R  U  U  C  M  N  I
S  P  O  W  E  R  F  U  L  W  E  Z
```

HUGE
IMMENSE
MASSIVE
MIGHTY
MONSTROUS
POWERFUL

REALLY BIG!

Help the **dog** visit the Taj Mahal.

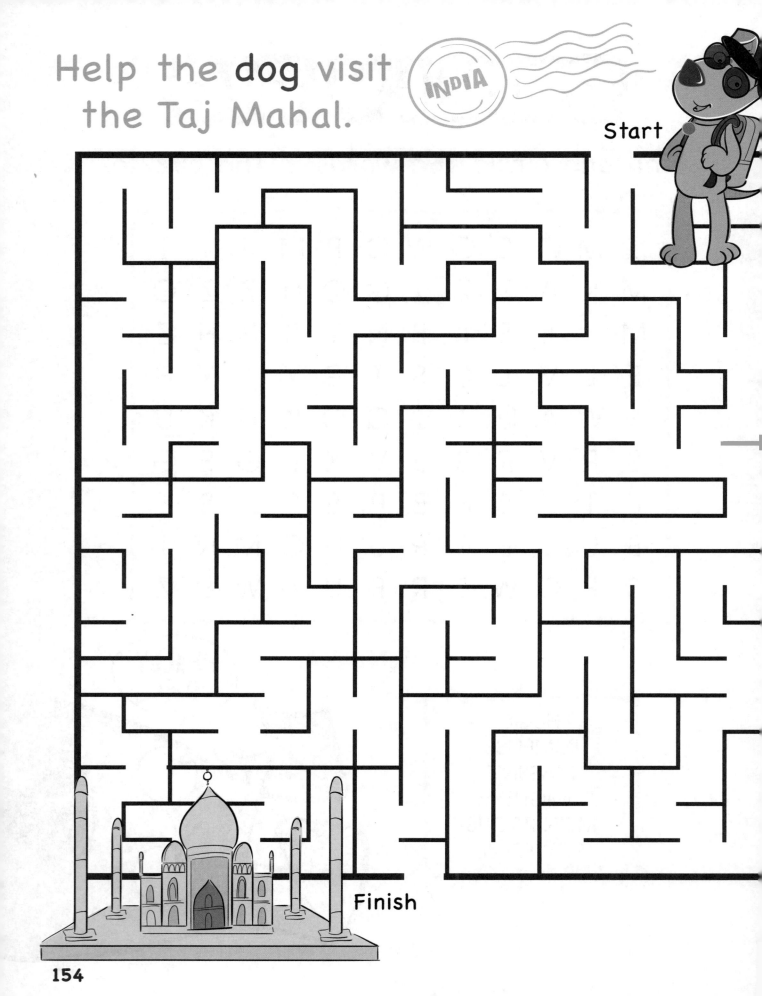

INDIA

Start

Finish

SHARE TWO LETTERS

Each word has two letters in common with the other words. Using the pictures as hints, fill in the rest of the words.

1.

2.

3.

4.

5.

6.

1. [ ] [ ] N D [ ]

2. [ ] [ ] N D

3. [ ] [ ] N D [ ] [ ]

4. [ ] N D

5. [ ] [ ] N D [ ] [ ]

6. [ ] [ ] N D [ ]

LUNCH LINE TREASURE HUNT

Find the **24** hidden items in the cafeteria next door.

- ❑ Paintbrush
- ❑ Feather
- ❑ Arrow
- ❑ Lemon Slice
- ❑ Basketball
- ❑ Open Book
- ❑ Bowl
- ❑ Sailboat
- ❑ Donut
- ❑ Grapes
- ❑ Sock
- ❑ Crown

- ❑ Acorn
- ❑ Popsicle
- ❑ Heart
- ❑ Mitten
- ❑ Snowman
- ❑ Flag
- ❑ Spoon
- ❑ Music Note
- ❑ Rake
- ❑ Ice Cream Cone
- ❑ Ring
- ❑ Pencil

TOY STORE

Use the word lists to fill out the grid below.
Hint: Count the squares in the grid first to
see where the words will fit.

3-Letters
buy
pay

4-Letters
shop
toys
sell
sale

5-Letters
games
music
guard
clerk
hobby

8-Letters
elevator

PUZZLE CLUES

Use the pictures as clues to fill in the crossword puzzle.

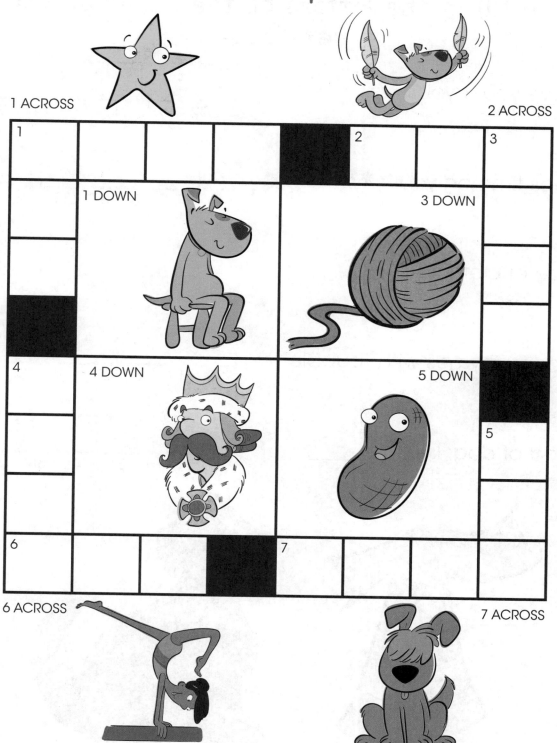

1 ACROSS

2 ACROSS

1 DOWN

3 DOWN

4 DOWN

5 DOWN

6 ACROSS

7 ACROSS

RIDDLE ME THIS

Use the word box on the next page to answer each clue in the squares. Then, use your answers to fill in the letters of the riddle on the next page.

a. Above your eyebrows

24	12	7	21	17	14	3	8

b. Keeps time on your wrist

1	28	37	11	2

c. Piece of clothing

16	46	43	39	31

d. Danger; rhymes with "bubble"

20	19	6	27	9	34	35

e. Breed of dog; Irish _____

45	10	36	4	38	22

f. Use to make a fire

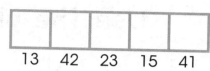

5	26	47	30

g. Slightly wet

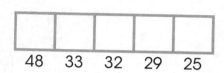

13	42	23	15	41

h. Rough and loud

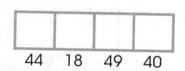

48	33	32	29	25

i. Little children; toddlers

44	18	49	40

trouble	tots
rowdy	forehead
watch	moist
wood	shirt
setter	

$\overline{1}$ $\overline{2}$ $\overline{3}$ $\overline{4}$ $\overline{5}$ $\overline{6}$ $\overline{7}$ 8 $\overline{9}$ $\overline{10}$ $\overline{11}$ $\overline{12}$ $\overline{13}$ $\overline{14}$ $\overline{15}$

$\overline{16}$ $\overline{17}$ $\overline{18}$ 19 $\overline{20}$ $\overline{21}$ $\overline{22}$ $\overline{23}$ $\overline{24}$ $\overline{25}$ $\overline{26}$ $\overline{27}$ $\overline{28}$ $\overline{29}$ $\overline{30}$

$\overline{31}$ $\overline{32}$ $\overline{33}$ $\overline{34}$ $\overline{35}$ 36 $\overline{37}$ $\overline{38}$ $\overline{39}$ $\overline{40}$ $\overline{41}$ $\overline{42}$ $\overline{43}$ $\overline{44}$?

$\overline{45}$ $\overline{46}$ $\overline{47}$ $\overline{48}$ $\overline{49}$.

PICTURE CLUES

Use the pictures as clues to fill in the crossword puzzle.

1 ACROSS

2 ACROSS

1 DOWN

3 DOWN

4 DOWN

5 DOWN

6 ACROSS

7 ACROSS

WATCHING WALKERS

What went wandering below?

SHARE TWO LETTERS

Each word has two letters in common with the other words. Using the pictures as hints, fill in the rest of the words.

1.

2.

1. | | | | O | T |

2. | O | T | | | |

3.

3. | | | O | T |

4.

4. | | O | T | |

5.

5. | | O | T | | |

6. | | O | T | | |

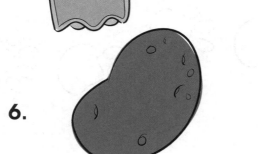

RHYME TIME

Using the pictures as hints, fill in the missing letters of the rhyming words.

S U N

P H O N E

C O R N

Answer Key

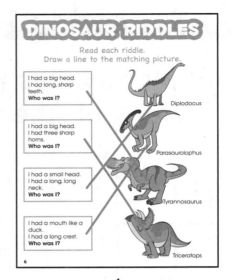

5

6

7

8

10

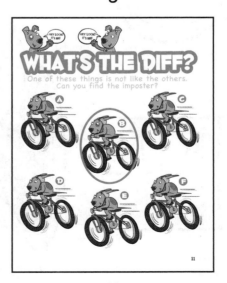

11

Answer Key

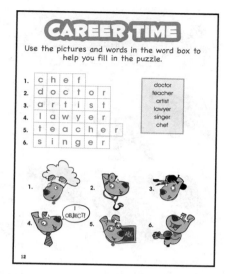

12

13

15

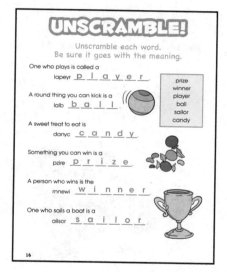

16

17

18

Answer Key

19

20

21

22

24

25

Answer Key

26

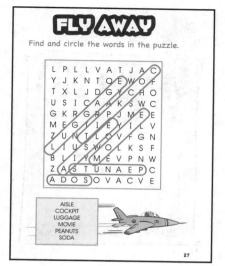

27

28

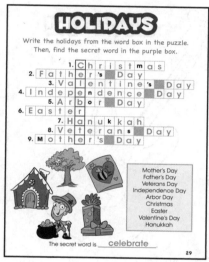

29

30

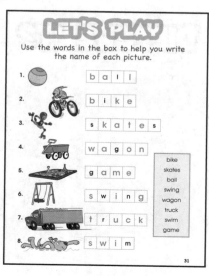

31

Answer Key

32

33

34

35

37

38

Answer Key

39

40

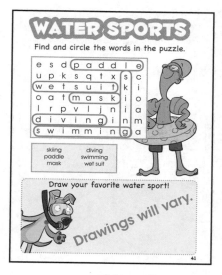

41

42

43

44

Answer Key

45

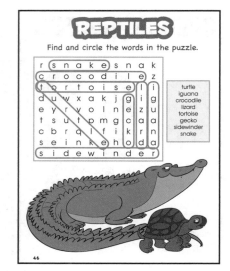

46

ANIMAL ANALOGIES

Use the word bank to help complete these analogies. An analogy is the expression of two like comparisons.

rattlesnake	cow	camel	elephant

A **hill** is to **land** as a **hump** is to a(n) **camel**

A **hand fan** is to a **human** as **ears** are to a(n) **elephant**

Four quarters are to a **dollar** as **four stomachs** are to a(n) **cow**

A **chest beat** is to a **gorilla** as a **shaking rattle** is to a(n) **rattlesnake**.

47

48

50

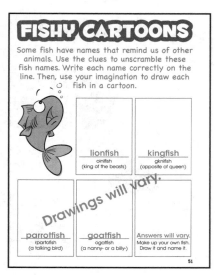

51

Answer Key

52

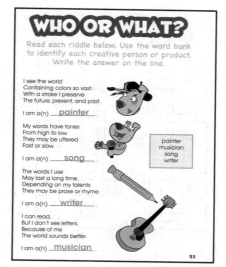

WHO OR WHAT?

Read each riddle below. Use the word bank to identify each creative person or product. Write the answer on the line.

I see the world
Containing colors so vast.
With a stroke I preserve
The future, present, and past.

I am a(n) __painter__

My words have tones
From high to low.
They may be uttered
Fast or slow.

I am a(n) __song__

word bank:
painter
musician
song
writer

The words I use
May last a long time.
Depending on my talents
They may be prose or rhyme.

I am a(n) __writer__

I can read,
But I don't see letters.
Because of me
The world sounds better.

I am a(n) __musician__

53

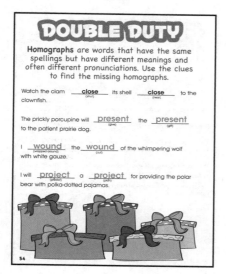

DOUBLE DUTY

Homographs are words that have the same spellings but have different meanings and often different pronunciations. Use the clues to find the missing homographs.

Watch the clam __close__ (shut) its shell __close__ (near) to the clownfish.

The prickly porcupine will __present__ (give) the __present__ (gift) to the patient prairie dog.

I __wound__ (wrapped around) the __wound__ (cut) of the whimpering wolf with white gauze.

I will __project__ (predict) a __project__ (plan) for providing the polar bear with polka-dotted pajamas.

54

UNDERWHATER?

What do you see under the sea?

Drawings will vary.

55

CRAZY WEATHER

Find and circle the words in the puzzle.

BLIZZARD
ICY
SLEET
SNOWY
STORMY
WINDY

```
D L I A S L E E T F
S J K C G M T W B T
K N Y W Y D I C O B
E Y O F L Y L L L X
F T J W A O D I D W
J S C Z Y W Z W M I
B I F D A Z H P N N
M M Y R A O M Z G D
S T O R M Y Z O N Y
F E D E D U F Y B H
```

Draw your favorite thing to do in the winter.

Drawings will vary.

56

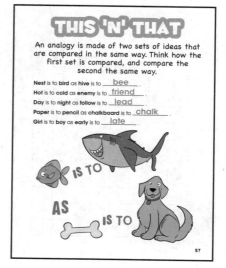

THIS 'N' THAT

An analogy is made of two sets of ideas that are compared in the same way. Think how the first set is compared, and compare the second the same way.

Nest is to **bird** as **hive** is to __bee__
Hot is to **cold** as **enemy** is to __friend__
Day is to **night** as **follow** is to __lead__
Paper is to **pencil** as **chalkboard** is to __chalk__
Girl is to **boy** as **early** is to __late__

IS TO

AS

IS TO

57

Answer Key

Help the friends catch some fireflies.

Start

Finish

58

58

SECRET MESSAGE

L + (✈ - j) + 's = __Let's__

S + (🐝 - b) = __see__

(🌳 - ree) + (🦆 - n) = __the__

(🌻 - t) + t + (🥜 - b) = __United__

(📎 - pler) + (⚫ - ir) + s = __States__

What is your favorite place in the United States? Draw a picture of it.

Drawings will vary.

59

59

60

GRAND CANYON

Complete each fact about the Grand Canyon by unscrambling the letters at the end of each sentence. Use the word bank if necessary.

| Mead | desert | Colorado |
| Arizona | deep | |

The canyon is between 4,000 and 5,000 feet __deep__. (epde)

The Grand Canyon is located in northwestern __Arizona__. (zanioar)

The canyon was formed by the __Colorado__ River. (rodoclao)

The bottom of the Grand Canyon is mostly __desert__. (seetrd)

The lake that forms at the southern end of the Grand Canyon is called Lake __Mead__. (deam)

What kind of animals do you think live in the Grand Canyon? Draw a picture of one.

Drawings will vary.

62

62

Follow the 🧦's to get the monster under the bed!

Start

Finish

63

63

JUMBLED DANGERS

Each set of jumbled letters below represents two possible dangers to explorers. Use the clue to help you unscramble the letters to name the two dangers. Use all the letters, but use each letter only once.

Clue: Both are cats, but one is "king."
PLEIALRONDO
__lion__   __leopard__

Clue: Both are man-eating and live in or near water.
PIROOEIACCRNDALH
__piranha__   __crocodile__

Clue: Both can make you "shake, rattle, and roll."
OEVLCTAUAHEORANQK
__earthquake__   __volcano__

Clue: Both like to "monkey around."
BLOBAOIOGRLAN
__baboon__   __gorilla__

What is a place you would like to explore? Draw a picture of this place.

Drawings will vary.

64

64

Answer Key

65

66

67

68

69

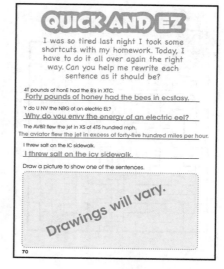

70

Answer Key

71

SPOOKY

Find and circle the words in the puzzle.

```
B P M Y X N H U T B F
O J J W I T C H R F U
S T F L X R E Y F L
C T B L A C K C A T L
N C A N D Y M Y E N M
A D K T U B R R I E O
S K E L E T O N A K O
E Z H X N A H L C C N
```

SKELETON   FULL MOON
BOO   CANDY
WITCH   BLACK CAT

Draw something spooky.

Drawings will vary.

72

Finish the poster!

WANTED

GLUNOX THE GREAT SPACEASE PIRATE

Drawings will vary.

73

OUT OF THIS WORLD

Design an alien space craft.

Drawings will vary.

74

Help the matador reach his bull.

Start

Finish

75

RIDDLE TIME

Use the word box on the next page to answer each clue in the squares on the right. Then, use your answers to fill in the letters of the riddle on the next page.

a. Not old
Y	O	U	N	G
38	34	40	25	48

b. _____ and thank you
P	L	E	A	S	E
45	42	20	14	32	7

c. Police _____
S	T	A	T	I	O	N
41	9	24	4	46	11	15

d. Tells the time
W	A	T	C	H
1	35	33	13	2

e. You smell with this
N	O	S	E
19	17	26	22

f. Long stream of water
R	I	V	E	R
23	10	21	37	36

g. Female nobility
Q	U	E	E	N
5	6	31	44	47

76

Answer Key

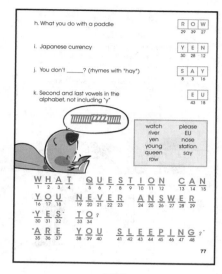

77

78

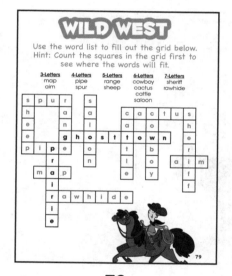

79

80

82

83

Answer Key

84

85

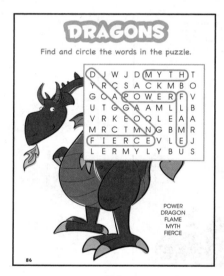

86

87

88

Answer Key

89

91

92

93

94

Answer Key

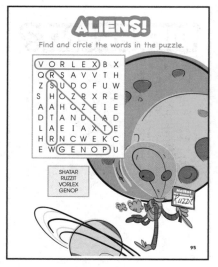

95

96

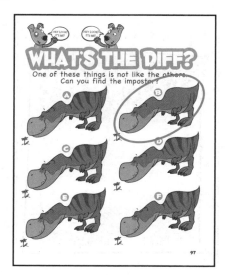

97

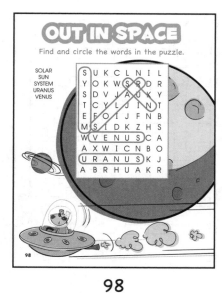

98

99

Answer Key

100

101

102

104

105

Answer Key

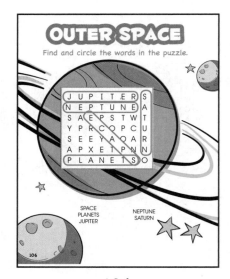

106

107

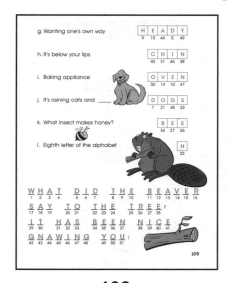

108

109

110

Answer Key

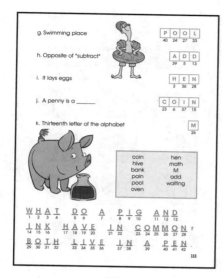

g. Swimming place — P O O L (40 24 27 33)

h. Opposite of "subtract" — A D D (39 5 13)

i. It lays eggs — H E N (2 36 28)

j. A penny is a _____ — C O I N (23 6 37 15)

k. Thirteenth letter of the alphabet — M (26)

coin	hen
hive	math
bank	M
pain	add
pool	waiting
oven	

W H A T   D O   A   P I G   A N D
1 2 3 4   5 6   7   8 9 10   11 12 13

I N K   H A V E   I N   C O M M O N ?
14 15 16   17 18 19 20   21 22   23 24 25 26 27 28

B O T H   L I V E   I N   A   P E N
29 30 31 32   33 34 35 36   37 38   39   40 41 42

111

112

113

114

Drawings will vary.

116

Answer Key

117

118

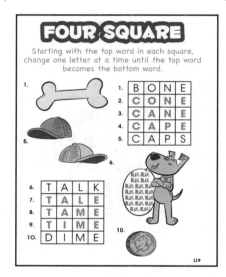

119

120

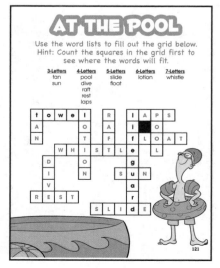

121

Answer Key

122

123

124

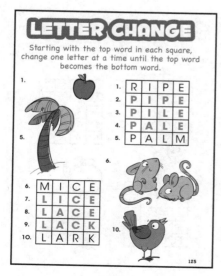

125

126

Answer Key

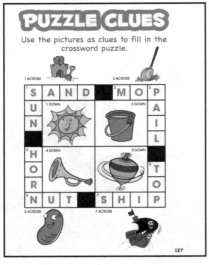

127

128

129

130

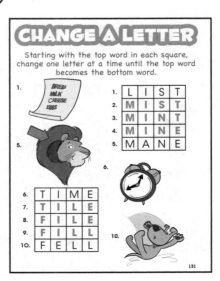

131

Answer Key

133

134

135

136

137

Answer Key

138

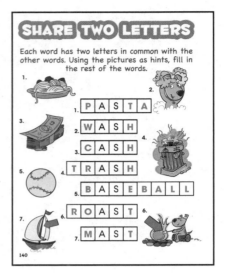

140

141

142

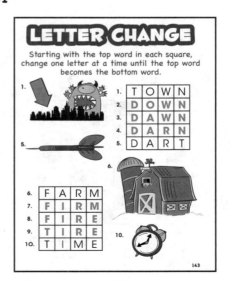

143

Answer Key

144

145

146

147

149

Answer Key

150

151

152

153

154

Answer Key

155

156

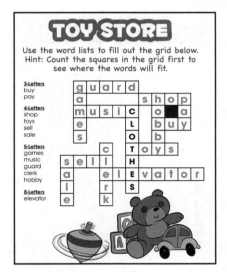

158

159

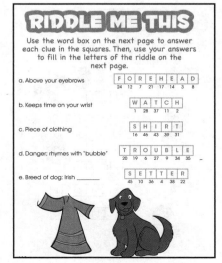

160

Answer Key

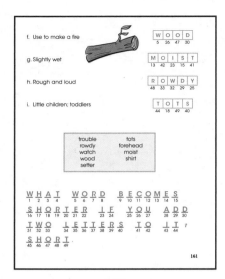

f. Use to make a fire — W O O D (5 26 47 30)

g. Slightly wet — M O I S T (13 42 23 15 41)

h. Rough and loud — R O W D Y (48 33 32 29 25)

i. Little children; toddlers — T O T S (44 18 49 40)

trouble	tots
rowdy	forehead
watch	moist
wood	shirt
setter	

W H A T   W O R D   B E C O M E S
1 2 3 4   5 6 7 8   9 10 11 12 13 14 15

S H O R T E R   I F   Y O U   A D D
16 17 18 19 20 21 22   23 24   25 26 27   28 29 30

T W O   L E T T E R S   T O   I T ?
31 32 33   34 35 36 37 38 39 40   41 42   43 44

S H O R T .
45 46 47 48 49

161

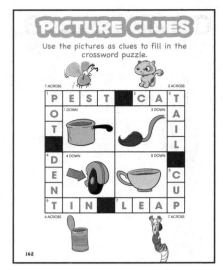

PICTURE CLUES

Use the pictures as clues to fill in the crossword puzzle.

162

WATCHING WALKERS

What went wandering below?

Drawings will vary.

163

SHARE TWO LETTERS

Each word has two letters in common with the other words. Using the pictures as hints, fill in the rest of the words.

1. C A R R O T
2. O T T E R
3. B O O T
4. P O T S
5. B O T T L E
6. P O T A T O

164

RHYME TIME

Using the pictures as hints, fill in the missing letters of the rhyming words.

S U N
R U N

B O N E
P H O N E

C O R N
H O R N

165